8 YEARS OF DISTRACTIONS

SUPRIYA SAIBA

INDIA • SINGAPORE • MALAYSIA

ISBN 979-8-89067-753-2

DEDICATION

I am indebted to my beautiful and selfless friends Keerthana, Moksha, Sharon, and Teja for always being supportive. This wouldn't be possible without them.

THE LIST OF POEMS

SYNOPSIS OF MY BOOK

People were mean, selfish, and unkind to her. They thought she was worthless, incapable, and unlucky.

When she was young, she was desperate, she was not aware of her surroundings, and she did not have confidence in herself, but she did know that she was going to overcome all of these one day.

She stood up for her, she spoke her heart out and finally, she is powerful.

-1-

JOURNEY

I sat beside an old man at a bus stop
And he says, "you'll be successful
And come meet me here one day,
I'll not go anywhere."

Getting into the bus,
More how far is it, mom?
When are we going to reach the place?

Interesting talks with strangers,
Exchanging contact numbers with them,
Meeting babies at the temple.

Traveling diverse places,
I discovered one common
thing is love.

Reaching home,
I asked my mother, "Again when?"

-2-

ON THE WAY

We will go for a ride,
Hold me tight,
It feels warm and safe,
My thoughts in the wind,
Secret conversations in the traffic,
Trust me nobody can hear it.

Empty roads with no blaring in my ears,
Sometimes roadblocks and road cracks,
In between, there's road rage.

Let's escape this city,
Get out of the reality
And find the ecstasy,
Moving away from the damage
And getting to destiny.

-3-

THE SILENT GIRL

The girl enters the classroom
And sits quietly,
Everyone in the class
Strangely stares at her,
She writes something
that no one understands,
And they laugh at her
And she smiles thinking
them as innocents.

The toughest problem with the
black ink on the white board,
Mean girls taunting her
for her outdated style.

People assume that knowing famous things
is a brilliance,
But she is busy in inventing something else.

Nobody comes to her
for the advice
Because it doesn't talk about revenge.

An uncontrollable girl comes to her
And says, “conquering harrow situations made me stronger”,
Though, benefiting from them should not shape you imperiously prouder.

The principal comes to the classroom,
Everyone tries to hide their face
Including the fierce girl
Except the silent girl.

-4-

IMMORAL ATTACHMENT

You and I caught staring
at each other at a hustling party,
he reads what's on my T-shirt,
he thinks that I'm not interested to talk
but hey, I'm interested.

He calls me to sneak out with him,
turns on the broken fan so that nobody can hear our unsure conversation.

Returning home by bus,
I'll talk with you on the call till I reach my home,
but the way you kissed me,
I'm sure that was not your first time.

Will you give me your weekends?
sorry, are my expectations on you too high?
but If I talk, you have to stop yourself
a thousand times!
We walk around the mall
he looks around
and doesn't hold my hand,

kisses with no flowers,
It is just a string attached,
fights for high demands.

This connection has started and ceased
without knowing anyone.

-5-

WHY WOULD YOU TALK WITH ME FOR HOURS?

He shares so many things with me
nonstopingly,
I thought he liked me,
But innocently, he just
brags things about himself,
Don't come to this unsafe reality,
You'll be demolished.

You never ask any superfluous questions to me,
You never reveal other people's secrets to me,
So I share mine with you faithfully.

One thing I liked most about him is
still he has not gotten his first kiss,
I'm envious of the fictional characters of girls that he creates in his story.

Apart from our work,
Can we talk about love and family?

How can you extend the conversations
without bringing up any topic?
If you think that we are just friends
then why would you talk with me for hours?

-6-

SIX FINGERS

I want somebody to say that I'm hurt
Even if I don't admit it,
The pain hasn't digested at all
Even after a long walk,
I can spot faults even with my poor eyesight,
She makes others worry
and grows her hair long.

The sketchy relationship, you didn't know
And also it didn't grow,
I couldn't able to hear you
because of the strong wind,
The sun came up immediately
after the heavy rain,
If it is painful now
then your progression is correct.

Carrying the purse of an innocent girl
Made me weaker,
I guess you will never remember me
while using my stolen things.

When playing handball, I want to use my foot,
When playing football, I want to use my hands.

Wanted to throw away the phone in the lake,
He looks like he smokes,
But If he touches it, he fixes it,
You were shocked when I said I was happy.

-7-

CRESTFALLEN ENDINGS

I haven't seen you here before,
Are you new to this town?
Staying opposite my house,
The sun from my window to your window.

Daily you never turn backside
While closing the gate
But this time you turned and looked at me.

You showed me
your amusing childhood photos,
And you told me a secret after your mom,
together we painted my bedroom walls,
Your mom says from the kitchen,
soon you all are going to visit the waterfall.

You said you're leaving for a trip for a week,
Your handshake says,
you don't want to leave me,
here I'm waiting for the next week
to arrive in minutes,
I've been waiting, waiting and waiting.

Today the window looks bored
without the sun in it,
There, do you hear my whispers in the waterfalls?

And the old man beside your house has said you've left the town forever.

And you came back home after years
By holding the other girl's hand,
But here,
I still keep your shabby photos,
the colours of my bedroom's wall
are still the same,
I haven't replaced them.

I stopped watching our favourite movie
because now we are not
those characters anymore.

-8-

EIGHT YEARS OF DISTRACTIONS

I can see that the door has not closed fully,
Now I have to get up and close it completely
As I don't let the sunshine in.

Did not study the whole night,
Blaming other things and wasting my time,
Expecting that my friend would help me with the exam.

Afraid to go out with my shameful exam results,
Scared to speak with strangers at the grocery store.

The internet world has closed the windows
In my room,
Talking with unknown lovely boys,
Writing romantic poems for them.

The beautiful present conversations rooted in deplorable past,
Wish I was conscious when I was sad.

-9-

I KNOW YOU LOVED ME

Did I just see him
Or was that just my assumption?
When we saw each other unexpectedly,
You dropped the milkshake from your hand,
You looked messy and unconfident.

You did not want to leave this place so quickly,
You did not want to end the conversation.

Flashback to when you met me,
You shared about your affectionate family,
As if you wanted to share the future with me,
And you did not do things
Which I did not like.

-10-

DEAR FRIEND

We don't want to hang up the call
even when we are done with the conversation,
I'll make fun of myself just to entertain you.

To make you feel comfortable,
I'd say I have the same problems as you have,
I'll make you feel casual
even if you cancel your plan to meet me,
That's okay when you left me at the bar alone.

You said your dad drinks alcohol,
To make you feel safe,
I'd say my father drinks alcohol too
when he doesn't even exist,
I'll make you feel unworried
even if you say you can't marry me.

We couldn't able to figure out things
Even after speaking for three long hours
But at least I can make a tea
And do the dishes for you, my friend.

-11-

CHANGES

Whom you called bitch when you were a kid,
Now she is your best friend.

A beautiful clock that I craved
for at the exhibition,
now it's a useless thing,
I was thrilled when I got a new cycle,
I don't know why did I cry for a lion toy,
Now I'm no more excited about the new things.

The one who was sitting beside me
during my school days is famous now.

His slang changes
She questions, "With whom you were"?
And got mystified about her boyfriend
And kisses two guys after her breakup.

A poor humble girl used to welcome us
with a broken door,
Now her guards open a gigantic gate for her,
So far life was unswerving for me,

till how many days will it stay?
and tomorrow it might be zigzag,
till how many days will it stay?
Promptly it will fade away.

Now I hear Wise words from brutal people,
The kid who was wild,
has become silent and quiet.

-12-

CHILDHOOD INSECURITIES

You'll judge the way I laugh
and say don't laugh like that
and make fun of how stupid
and weird I look
When my teeth are visible.

Are dead souls gonna watch me being naked?
Did I greet my relatives properly?
Am I sitting properly without any intimate body part getting exposed?

-13-

A SUDDEN CHANGE ON A BIG DAY

You spoke about your abusive mother,
You cried with me,
Wanted to leave the house,
We've built a house under my bed.

A grand wedding day,
You're dancing with your husband,
Now you are making fun of my dreams with your husband.

Before you were with me
sharing your sadness,
Now you are busy
sharing your happiness with others,
I forgot that you give
the same love to everyone.

-14-

LIGHTS OUT

You share the rain there,
I share the sun here,
Well, we don't share the same time,
It's unequal,
But we do share similar problems,
But when are we going to be joyous?
When do the problems stop for us?

The guy who said you are my world,
Invited other planets,
when are we going to talk
about our new delightful moments, my friend?
As we are still floating in the murky water.

I call you when there is a
blackout in my village
And you bring dazzling warmth, my friend.

-15-

UNNECESSARY SENSATION

You look rich with the artificial jewelry
But not beautiful,
Cruel laughs with your friends,
Your team attacking me,
Spreading unwarranted news
And celebrating that I don't deserve the trophy,
So early they're relishing me as a loser
But I'll become that
For which you laughed it
As a joke.

-16-

THE GORGEOUS GIRL IN THE CITY

Her innocence made me spellbound,
Her sparkling nose pin,
When she bends her head down,
I see the reflection of the nose pin
Dazzling in her eyes,
The rose will be upset
If she doesn't touch it.

Please don't leave me
If a boy joins our conversation
And nobody cared
When I silently left the room.

-17-

HEY WARM GUY

We don't care about veracious love,
Let the nutty world think we did not grow,
We believe it's a spontaneous love affair
But the world thinks it's for obnoxious gratification.

I appreciate you for not looking sincerely into my eyes,
But between us, not everything is forever existent.

His voice is like a delicate wine glass,
Falling off without any pieces left on the floor,
My hair touching his face
And heaven is with me,
It feels better not to have any love battling emotions
When there are other helpless vehemence are shattering,
Promise me will you keep our relationship confidential?

-18-

IMBALANCE PERIOD

I came across you through one person,
Maybe we got tied up for some reason,
You're something different,
the grace you carry in your alluring eyes,
A funny persona with an interesting outlook, made me questionable,
Those eyes of pearls rays falling
into my slaughtered eyes
to give them rise.

Our closeness seemed like we were together for sixty years
But haplessly I'm here to tell you that somebody wants to be yours.

My unexplainable caged love for someone is stuck for us,
Escaping that ended euphoric.

Bravely buried the alive past,
I did not notice that
I fell in love with you unknowingly,
But my innocent heart connected to yours knowingly.

You with seriousness
and love restrictions around you,
Can never be mine,
Standards on your dream girl were pretty high
and those gesticulations waved me bye-bye.

I see the past and present, my reverence for you was constant,
Now I see the future, it says "Our relationship can't stand",
Wish I could share my fondness for you directly
Since my heart can't bear you saying "sorry".

-19-

OLD DUSTY THINGS

Summer holidays,
Empty grounds,
Children on television,
Melted ice-creams,
Well, I've grown old,
Grew up with gadgets,
The streets are not healthy
Without trees,
Internet wires occupied
all over the buildings,
Found the toys that I made
after coming home from school,
The dust on the letters
that I wrote for my friend,
The words got faded away
But the promises were loyal,
The stapler with full pins
Got rust in it,
My favorite outfit
Has lost its color,
Plastic flowers look
fresh and shiny
like false people.

-20-

WANDERING AROUND WITH EMPTY HANDS

He's not ready to hold my hand
but his actions sometimes mystify me,
does he love me or not?
Those nights when I told you
that I liked you,
you had put me in the place
and I don't know where am I.

My friend found you
Crestfallen when I blurted out that
I liked you
then I talked to you
but you were not excited,
I was happy that the reason was not me
and was sad because you were sad.

I never expect him
to do fine things,
I admire him for whatever he does.

I never become lonesome
without your warmth
Because you are my blessing,
Never a distress.

Looking you from far away
you look achievable,
makes me cheerful
rather than waiting for your answer.

-21-

KISS

Me, sitting on a bench
in an empty bus stop,
waiting for you
And you found me through the map
written in your palm.

We're in the theatre,
I glanced at you
and it rained diamonds
when I looked into your eyes
then I looked backside
and there was a gunfire.

Sitting on your scooter,
closer to your back,
and i pulled myself backward
and felt, how barbarous it was
without a kiss.

Going back home,
arguing with him over the phone,
and I'm envious of the things
that you touch.

-22-

THEY LOST ME

Please, even I want to come to the mall,
Take me there,
I saw a little kid's mother asking her,
"Do you want more toys?"
The kid's dad bought costly icecream for her
And I was staring at the window.

I was with my family,
All of a sudden I was missed in the crowd
And I found them at the magic show,
I was missed again,
This time it was planned
And not my mistake.

-23-

DYING WHILE LIVING

Everybody in the hall sleeping peacefully,
I'm in my room sitting
and breathing heavily,
Fickle thoughts and wheezing sounds,
the raindrops on the dried leaves
When the roots have already swallowed up
the poisonous drink,
Dying while living,
So far I'm living while dying.

-24-

LUCK IS A MYTH

Isn't it dejecting losing the match
even after practicing for several months?

It's like a ludo game,
The dice number is a fate
But it depends on how sharply we have
To make our next move.

She isn't fortunate to get the glory,
Her steps were just clever.

-25-

IN THE MIDDLE OF THE GAME

Everyone's eyes were on me
When I joined in the middle of the game,
Did they think am I going to drop the ball?
Neither I did not come here to lose the game.

No rudimentary skills at an early age,
Innocent with no training,
Brutal people say,
If not practiced since childhood
means you can't master,
So do you think did I enter the game to get eliminated?

-26-

A MORNING WALK WITH MY GRANDPA

A giant neem tree in front of our house,
Gives a pleasant air when people feel drowsy,
Full of green grass covered the ground,
Walking into the razor grass
to the open clean grounds.

Me wearing the same old
faded frayed blue T-shirt
And My grandpa's walking with a broken bone.

In the middle of the way,
We look at the sky and talk;
space, planets, sun, moon
and get lost in the black hole
But when we come back to the reality,
We feel stupid about the norms of the world.

Switching lanes change our topic,
I say, "You are growing old day by day
So are your repeated stupid jokes ",
We reach the open clean ground,

We warm up and stretch our weaknesses,
And we bring the milk from the cowherd.

Walking back home,
We step from dark to light.

Other lovely uncles pass from us
And say, "Hey, you are too early today"
And we giggle looking at each other.

Reaching home,
Insects welcome us
when we enter the garden,

We made a route unknowingly
by walking through the grass daily.

-27-

MEDDLING PEOPLE

People say I have confusion
But those innocents don't know what's my final decision,
I'll be mindful when you put me on the spot,
You need not tell me where I lost
Because My dreams are like a trailer for my upcoming day,
I don't run my machine on others' saying,
I'm not a criminal to take your judgments.

I never get inspired by others
Because I know I'm not going to grow more than them,
I shun fancy things
as my problems are much more lavish than them.

Later I'll not get excited about thrashing you
Because I was already thrilled that my plans are going to work on you.

-28-

CUNNING GIRL

She comes to the class as a ruler
with her perfect ironed uniform
and polished shoes,
shamelessly lifting the skirts
of the other girls
might makes her cool,
I guess her parents at home
did not teach her
that getting good grades is not enough.

You stole my mate from my team
because you were too afraid
that you might lose the game.

-29-

BETRAYAL

Secrets pass from one to another
and reaches out to me steadily
because your dupe friends are
my hidden friends,
foolish title-tattling about me
is a dangerous thing for you,
I flirt with your boyfriend
and he likes it too
and shares all the disguised
items you carry in your handbag,
I know your clever plans
Because I had played your role once.

The mysterious things rotate
and I'm the criminal,
unfortunately, you could not encounter
that being extremely pleasant is treacherous,
I formed the group
and I can dismantle it too.

-30-

AM I NOT ENOUGH FOR YOU?

You built the castle for us,
thinking that it was fulfilled,
and need not to protect it,
and it's got dust,
and the spider created its web in the wall,
and the spider is that guiltless girl,
I'm so tired of cleaning it alone.

She says goodnight to me
and secretly begins her
private show, all-night,
and you are on the list,
she detests love
as she has to stick to only one.

Let them think that I'm a fool,
when I already know
what's happening in another room.

I can understand
your hurry replies for me,
like controlling the see-saw,

thinking yourself as a genius,
balancing the two.

You may think that I'm deranged
but the rules won't change,
One: I begged you once
Two: I warned you twice
Four: you'll see me fire the fort.

-31-

MY FRIENDS ARE IN LOVE

Her shaky hands on his shoulder
with hopefulness,
the confidence in her touch is pretty new,
secret hand gestures from long distances,
I'm curious have they hung out before?

In the car, he's playing music
by gazing at her,
he acts crazy
when she's not around.

She's been holding his drink outside the mall
and waiting for him,
I could not hold it any longer,
So I asked, are you in love?
And she blushed and ran away from us.

-32-

LATE NIGHT CHAT TILL 3 AM

Low brightness on the phone,
your messages sound mystical,
Feeling hungry at 2 am.

The power's gone,
everything's dark,
dogs bark,
beautiful things look scarier in the dark,
We came out and waved at each other.

I texted you saying, "I love you",
I suddenly woke up in the morning
and found out that it was a dream.

-33-

UNDER YOU

I'm frightened to say a word,
there are a lot of things I want to spill out
but I can't
because I'm under you.

That little innocent girl can't say no
to anyone,
she lies about her complications
because she is tired of answering your exaggerated questions.

When you spelled her name in the list,
you spelled her name with a signal to target,
maybe you'll know your capacity
when you take revenge on her.

Here, I can't say a word
that's greater than my standards,
my words would be worthless to you
as I'm voicing from the corner of
my unpainted house.

-34-

THE HIERARCHY SYSTEM

God is somebody that I don't know
And I don't believe
But people worship and admire God,
God might have said love is combining
unequal people to equals,
God might have never said, "Only this particular status people should worship me",
But God might have said
that I'm for everybody,
God might have said that every individual
has the right to do anything with their lives without harming anyone.

People have divided themselves from
the top hierarchy to the lowest,
Parents say you can't marry that person
Because they do not belong to our standards
But people believe in God and worship God,
People are hypocrites.

For what people are excessively overjoyed
by their status,
It will be demolished in the future,
For sure,
For sure,
And for sure.

-35-

A WILD GUY

He sits in the library for me
and says he's searching for other things,
he doesn't like the third person
to join our conversation.

He doesn't disturb me at the weekends,
he calls only me when he reaches home,
thank you for letting me speak about my day when you finished saying about yours.

At the temple, You gazed at me
after worshiping the god.
when I ask, "Do you love me"?
he shyly says, "I don't know".
now I know the answer.

-36-

CELEBRATING SOME BREAKING UP THINGS

Let him be excited about his new job,
Let him be excited with his new squad,
But he said that he had come
to this place for me,
Was that real?
Such a liar.

You did not tell me
that you've watched the new movie,
my whole life's been testing you.

The stains on the walls are proof
that how much we fought last night.

-37-

WHERE DID YOU GO AFTER POURING SO MUCH LOVE?

Weren't we delighted to catch up?
didn't we share the conversation
that we missed for two years?
that covered the entire two decades
but that excitement lasted
only for two months.

When I say goodbye,
you make all the love, the whole night,
and the next morning you stay as usual.

I want to run away with you to see
the mountains, sky, beach,
And nature by holding your hand,
Although, it feels silly for you,
but you come to see my body
even if it's a haunted place.

I said, "I'm in your town
and want to see your face",

then waited for you
at the bus stop for hours
and you simply said to leave the place.

We're on the bus,
sitting together,
you wanted to get off the next stop,
I held your hands
and said, "Please don't go"
but you didn't let me sit beside you
till the last stop.

-38-

SHATTERING SCHOOLS

Selfish girls refused to share
their notes with me,
it's better to play alone rather
than an unfair game,
I don't learn anything additional
for which I have to spend money,
the teachers watering the students
when they were already rained
and plucking them too soon
before its blossom,
everyone chose their friends
based on the grades,
the one who looks mad from the outside
is intelligent from the inside,
They didn't know that
I was making weapons at home,
Miss, please don't compare
my sports skills with the studies,
You know that I'm true
But you still detest me.

-39-

WE DROVE SO FAR AND RETURNED WITH EMPTY HANDS

I told you to leave
Because you were afraid
of your family and I was not
And I was afraid of the world and you were not,
You always talk about your dreams
But you never let me talk about mine,
I don't savour a cigar
but still, I kissed your smoked lips.

When we met after a long time,
You began the conversation
with your achievements,
you were afraid that if you tell the truth,
I might reject you.

When you are angry with me,
you call me by my real name,
I can understand your emotion
when you roughly closed the door.

I remember when you said,
“your problems are my problems”.
You did not spend time with me
in the name of saying “we will stay forever”.

Your brother helped us
getting out of our family problems,
now I put my head down
when we walk across each other,
our connection was like a plant,
It must grow vigorously by rain,
not by others watering us.

-40-

WINSOME BOY

I fancy the way you stretch your body,
your eyes make the alert whistle
to grab all the girl's attention,
handball game sweats
on your tired body made you
double ravishing.

The moment we looked at each other,
the first raindrop in my eye
made me wink at you,
rain hitting the ground like drums,
trees swinging like a violin.

My chattering stops
when you enter the hustling room
And just sitting at the corner
and waiting for your compliment.

When you came for me
by leaving the other girls,
it left them with jealousy
then with a cute smile

you ask them for mercy,
you asking me questions,
I almost forget the language to answer.

At night, you'll never let me sleep
Because those fantasy thoughts make me think about you
very deeply,
just looking at your face,
my eyes will never blink,
with that, I'll never get sick.

I'm just scared that I might fall in love with you
Because here you make me forget my love for a while
and I swear not to feel that again,
five minutes of colossal feelings stay temporarily
But you'll always be remembered in my story.

-41-

ALL ALONE

Covering my body,
Sneaking inside the blanket,
Scared of the ghosts,
I barely sleep at three or four
then I sleep very tightly as I'm no more.

The big spider that I've ever seen before
Even on the discovery channel,
It is coming near my legs,
All of a sudden I woke up
from the dreadful dream.

I slept again,
This time, My bed was moving round and round
As if I'm sitting in a merry-go-round,
I can hear the whispers of the ghost
But I'm unable to come out of the dream.

Woke up suddenly for a spider was a real fear
But I did not wake up for the ghost
was a fake fear.

I wake up in the morning,
I see no one in the house.

-42-

MY OUTRAGED GRANDMA

When I ask her for one Dosa,
She gives me two,
I can't find my things without her company,
During the night, her bangles sound
From another room
Make me feel that I'm not alone,
Her curse is my bliss,
Crying in the corner of the room
Because of her wise scoldings
And her sari flew to me
To wipe out my tears.

-43-

WE ARE NOT BUDDIES ANYMORE

Both of our families
were gossiping hilariously about people,
I was sitting beside my mum
And he was inside busy playing games on his computer,
His mother shouted at him to play with me,
He came out of his room awkwardly,
And we were pushed to talk forcefully.

Sitting together, talking about
our different school worlds,
And sharing dreams,
He introduced me to his squad,
Together we all made a strong bond.

Our little innocent minds didn't know
what are problems,
As kids, we were only focused on our dreams.

All of a sudden, one girl took him off with her by closing
my heart door,
He got to leave as his mum told him,
Deep down, my heart turned dim.

Slowly things were going worse,
our parents slowly stopped talking
and got into fights.

We two were left all alone in our homes,
as we were under our parents as slaves,
my mom warned me not to play with him again.

I think of it when we were nice buddies,
At the unexpected time, we two were separated from our families.

-44-

UNMANAGEABLE LIFE

You'll pretend to be busy
when you don't have money
to hang out with friends.

Would you be my lover for an hour?
I'm tired of acting like sober,
Why do we need to worry in this world
that we have created?

Living under the roof
with inadequate imagination,
stepped out to see the unbounded space.

I put my to-do list on my bed
before sleeping,
I have an answer
but you may not understand my steps.

It feels miserable when somebody is so good to you and unfavorable to others.

-45-

A FAKE FRIEND

Your pessimistic replies
even for tiny things,
impossible signs to my new plans
and with your crooked face,
you say, "That's not going to work",
Maybe at the end, you wanted
me to feel like a jerk.

When my rivals talk about me,
You don't say any word
Because you don't want to spoil your name,
this shows how brutally and safely
you play the game.

You kept me aside for a while
Since my standards were not fine.

What kind of a person are you?
Whose afraid to talk to me with your
restricted surroundings,
this messed up our strong bonding.

In front of everybody,
you abuse me very smartly
in the name of love,
Foolishly, I assumed it was with affection
But it was not.

In the past,
A Few people inserted knives in my heart
and it's still bleeding
then you came and touched it,
Now it's paining more.

-46-

THE WORLD

Viruses made us perceive
That we are connected,
If one country's infected,
It spreads throughout the entire world,
Developed or underdeveloped,
Just like our bodies,
If the leg's broken
Then the entire body has to suffer.

Nowhere on the trees,
is written that I belong to
the specific status or gender
as it is written on the products
And people's minds.

The law with immutable rules
that don't understand real emotions,
A politician stoushing with the opponent
party instead of struggling for the country.

Soon the butterflies turned into
mosquitoes in the streets.

-47-

UNUSUALITIES

I was not a cool girl at school,
I always stood outside the classroom,
I hated studies too,
I was only interested in sports,
And I didn't have dreams like other girls,
Everybody was unrelated to me.

Maybe you liked me without
knowing anything about me
and you might change,
I am neither smart to understand you,
I'm very little, maybe I'll learn things in future.

I say every individual is equal,
Now everybody is disconnected from me.

-48-

I AM TRYING

Walking through the streets
with my head down,
I can't look at a person straight into their eyes,
The monster girl at school pulls up the innocent girl's skirt,
Well, I can only defeat her in my dreams.

I can't look at someone when they're
counting money,
I could not able to sit comfortably
with a boy on the school bus,
My teacher slapped me in the face
to be assertive.

-49-

ALL AT A TIME

Unable to see vibrant colors,
touching my hand is making me scared,
So many hands in front of me,
Don't know which one to pick,
Picked up the useless call from far away,
Refused to make tea
when my sister was awake,
An innocent guy didn't judge me
When I'm going crazy in the bar.

To the questions I ask,
You answer it on the walls
to make it visible to the public
that how stupid I am,
I can feel you even in the dark
through your breath.

-50-

INDOLENT LIVING

The new opportunities approach
But no one supports,
Later, it's useless to expect the best
When the performance was already wretched,
I got sick of finding positivity everywhere.

When I got dismantled in front of everyone
then you've realized that I've been suffering from the past.

Waking up with the phone calls,
empty stomach,
and heavy thoughts in my brain,
going to bed for an unworried sleep
But I'm unable to relax even in my dreams.

I go out to hang out with my friends,
Classy restaurants, detrimental food,
And I come home and sleep alone in the bed,
But my grandma makes tasty food at home.

When I feel the pain of the wound on my hand,
I forget to appreciate how powerful my hand is,
Been sitting under the roof for a while
And the outdoor breeze is liberation and boundless.

www.ingramcontent.com/pod-product-compliance
Lightning Source LLC
LaVergne TN
LVHW010500160826
845677LV00012B/2569